Alice Chadwick

Birds & Butterflies

Colouring for mindfulness

hamlyn

An Hachette UK Company
www.hachette.co.uk

First published in France in 2015 by Éditions Marabout

This edition published in Great Britain in 2015 by
Hamlyn, a division of Octopus Publishing Group Ltd
Carmelite House
50 Victoria Embankment
London
EC4Y 0DZ
www.octopusbooks.co.uk

ISBN 978-0-600-63209-2

A CIP catalogue record for this book is available from the British Library.

Printed and bound in Italy

10 9 8 7 6 5 4 3

Illustrations: Alice Chadwick
Editorial Coordination: Catie Ziller
Design: Frédéric Voisin
Translation: JMS Books LLP (www.jmswords.com)
Assistant Production Manager: Caroline Alberti

Acknowledgements to:
Emmanuel and Catie
Special thanks to S, G & P

This book has been coloured in by:

....

Try to find the following...

1 bear

2 lighthouses

1 aeroplane

1 ladybird

1 chrysalis

1 moon

1 dragon

2 earrings

2 bees

3 keys

1 hat

2 snails

1 rainbow

1 beetle

4 shells

1 clock

1 strawberry

2 kites

1 cricket

2 bulbs

1 flock of sheep

4 boomerangs

1 umbrella

5 hearts

4 rings

1 ball

1 stone

1 seal

2 frogs

1 baby

1 globe

1 spider

1 pair of sugar tongs

2 gloves

1 button

1 goose quill

1 coin

1 walking stick

If you can't find some of the hidden objects, turn to the index at the end of the book to discover their whereabouts.

Within the pages of this book you will discover a wonderful world in black and white full of flying creatures: majestic butterflies, seagulls and eagle owls, parrots and peacocks, together with swallowtail butterflies and moths.

Along your journey of discovery you will encounter different plants and flowers as well as more unexpected objects, such as keys and jewellery or perhaps even a seal or a dragon.

Enjoy the search. Give your imagination free rein — let it take flight!

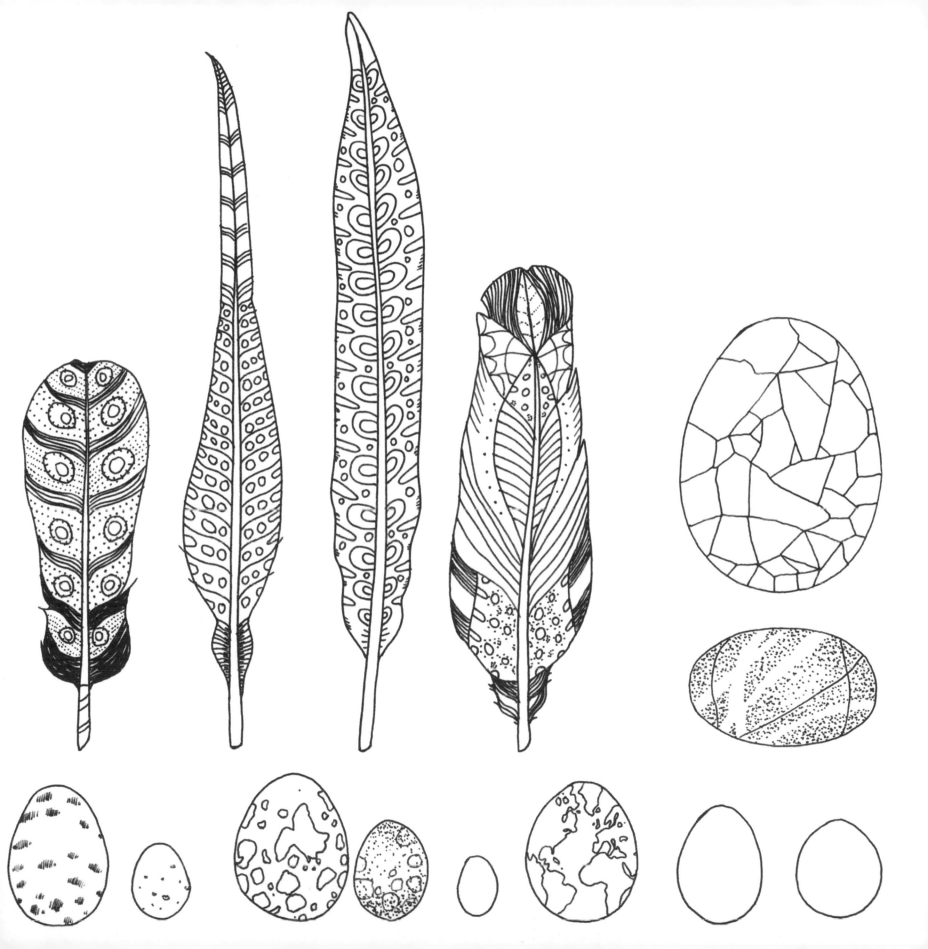

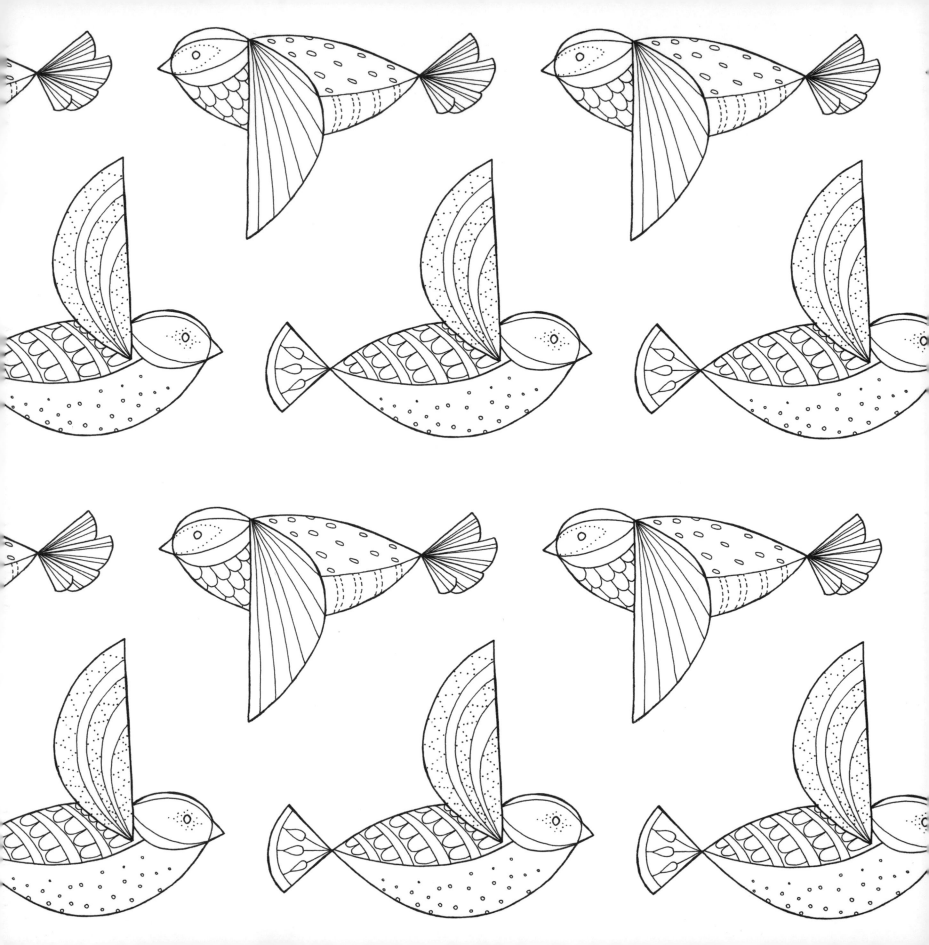

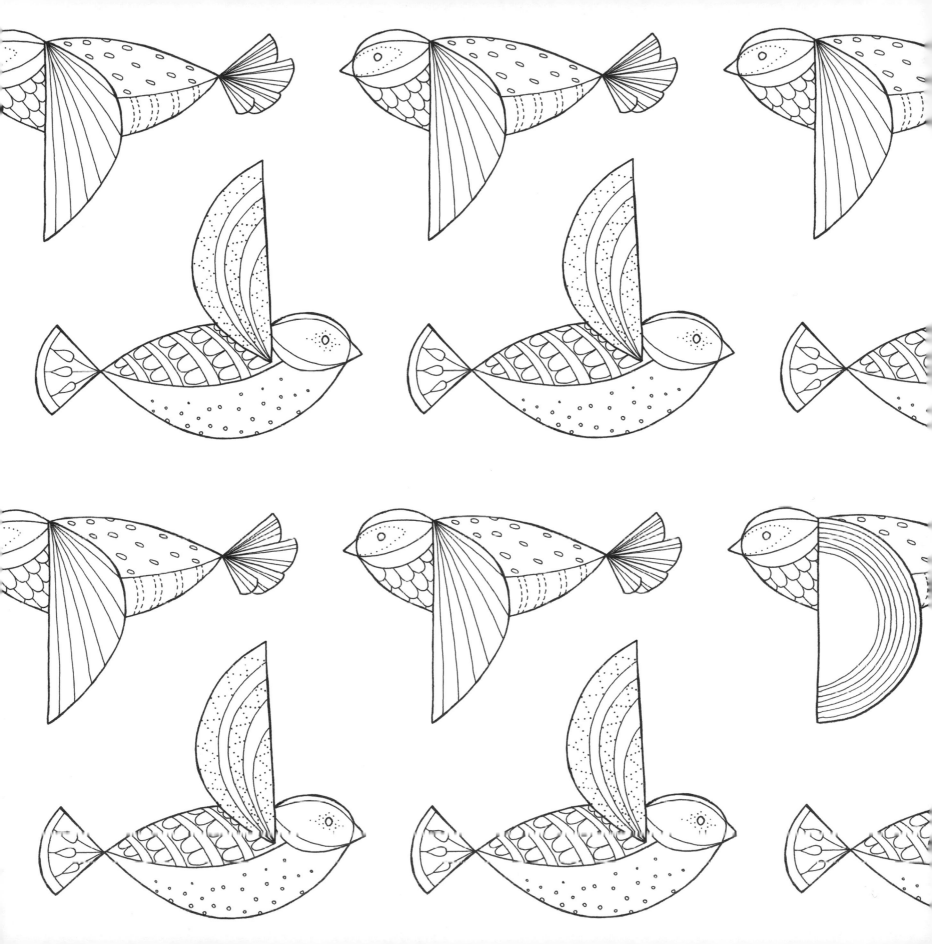

The hidden objects are...

1 chrysalis

4 boomerangs

1 coin

1 beetle

1 ball

4 hearts & 1 button

1 frog

1 cricket

1 clock

1 frog

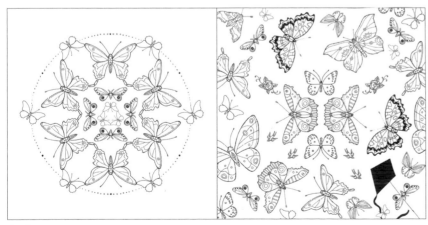

1 kite

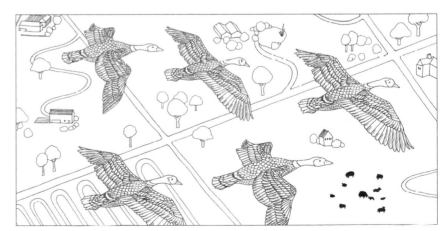

1 flock of sheep

1 umbrella

1 glove

1 pair of sugar tongs

4 rings

4 shells

1 hat & 2 bees

1 glove

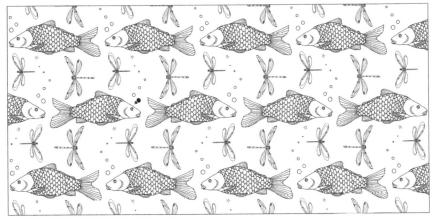

1 earring

1 bear

1 kite

1 ladybird

1 moon

1 dragon

2 lighthouses

1 heart

1 baby

3 keys

1 bulb

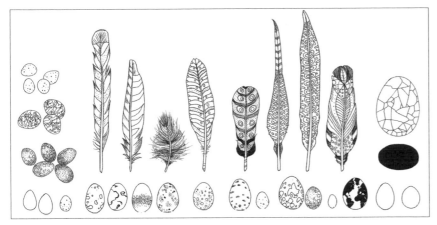

1 globe & 1 stone

1 snail

1 spider

1 walking stick

1 aeroplane

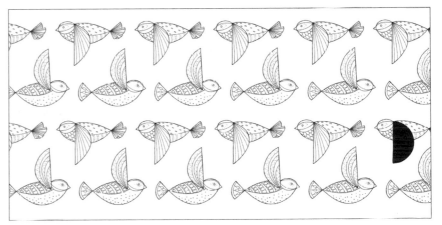

1 rainbow

1 strawberry

1 seal

1 bulb

1 earring

1 goose quill

1 snail